BIBLE **STUDY**
7 SESSIONS FOR SMALL GROUP AND PERSONAL USE

Acts 13-28
TO THE ENDS OF THE EARTH

CWR

Christine Platt

Copyright © CWR 2011

Published 2011 by CWR, Waverley Abbey House, Waverley Lane, Farnham, Surrey GU9 8EP, UK. Registered Charity No. 294387. Registered Limited Company No. 1990308.

Reprinted 2018, 2020.

The right of Christine Platt to be identified as the author of this work has been asserted by her in accordance with the Copyright, Designs and Patents Act 1988, sections 77 and 78.

All rights reserved. No part of this publication may be reproduced, stored in a retrieval system, or transmitted, in any form or by any means, electronic, mechanical, photocopying, recording or otherwise, without the prior permission in writing of CWR.

For a list of National Distributors, visit cwr.org.uk/distributors

Unless otherwise indicated, all Scripture references are from the Holy Bible: New International Version (NIV), copyright © 1973, 1978, 1984 by the International Bible Society.

Other versions are marked:

The Message: Scripture taken from The Message. Copyright © 1993, 1994, 1995, 1996, 2000, 2001, 2002. Used by permission of NavPress Publishing Group.

Extract on page 20 taken from the song 'How Deep the Father's Love' by Stuart Townend. Copyright © 1995 Thankyou Music. Adm. by worshiptogether.com songs excl. UK & Europe, adm. by kingswaysongs.com tym@kingsway.co.uk. Used by permission.

Concept development, editing, design and production by CWR

Cover image: istock/Mark Wragg and Bora Uçak

Printed in the UK by Kingsway CLC Trust

ISBN: 978-1-85345-592-6

Contents

5	Introduction
9	Week One **Let's go!**
15	Week Two **Disaster averted**
21	Week Three **Europe responds to the gospel**
27	Week Four **The persecuted Church blossoms**
33	Week Five **Faith under fire**
39	Week Six **Interacting with movers and shakers**
45	Week Seven **God's in charge!**
51	Leader's Notes

Introduction

From the Church's tumultuous birth in Jerusalem at Pentecost, the gospel has now spread throughout Jerusalem, Judea and Samaria (with small forays into parts of Asia), in keeping with the risen Jesus' prophecy (Acts 1:8). Luke recounts that story in Acts 1–12 (see *Acts 1–12: Church on the move*).[1] Luke now turns his attention to the regions beyond – 'the ends of the earth'.

Two significant conversions set the scene for global expansion. One is that of Saul, who later was called Paul, and who was commissioned as the apostle to the Gentiles (Acts 9). The other of Cornelius (Acts 10), one of the first Gentile converts. He met the Saviour through the apostle Peter, who needed a lot of persuasion to recognise the Gentiles as co-heirs of salvation!

Luke shifts the spotlight from Peter to Paul. By this time Paul was an acknowledged leader and teacher in the Antioch church. The city of Antioch was highly cosmopolitan – a glorious blend of cultures and people groups. The church there was already an example of unity – worshipping and serving together – in this cultural, racial and social mix. This was an ideal centre from which the Holy Spirit could launch the gospel to the vast unreached populations of Asia and Europe.

The key figure in chapters 13–28 is Paul, along with various team members. Although he is centre stage, he rarely travelled alone. At times Luke accompanied him. One can envisage Luke scribbling notes en route, collecting material for his Gospel and this book of Acts which links the Gospels and the Letters. Paul wrote his letters during his travels and especially during his various imprisonments. Luke was an eyewitness of many of the events and a trusted friend of Paul who knew his mind and heart. He was well qualified to write an accurate account.

Acts 13-28

The second part of Acts covers Paul's three missionary journeys. We can observe his strategy for urban evangelism and catch his heartbeat for pastoral care of these fledgling churches. We also see his wisdom in striving to get the Christian faith accepted as legal under the Roman administrative system. Rome as the epicentre of the Roman world drew him like a magnet. In his mind a vibrant church in Rome would spread the gospel throughout the known world. However, his journey to Rome was fraught with danger, catastrophe and hindrances, yet God miraculously got him there, albeit as a prisoner.

Acts contains mighty challenges to today's Church.

> the early church presents a radical community where the members held all things in common... a church that proclaimed Christ as supreme Lord with conversion in view... a church that depended on the Holy Spirit and gave top priority to prayer and moral purity... a church that took on suffering for the cause of Christ and considered it a basic ingredient of discipleship.[2]

It is sometimes tempting to read the events in Acts as things that happened a long time ago, having little or no relevance to the complex world in which we live today. Maybe we feel we can't identify with Paul or any of the giants of faith whom we read about. It's true that we do need to exercise discernment as we read and study, but 'Every part of Scripture is God-breathed and useful one way or another – showing us truth, exposing our rebellion, correcting our mistakes, training us to live God's way. Through the Word we are put together and shaped up for the tasks God has for us' (2 Tim. 3:16, *The Message*).

So, wherever we are on our journey with Jesus, Acts has important lessons for us. Acts shows us how Jesus started His Church and enabled it to spread. We in our day still live under the prophecy and commandment of Acts 1:8. We are to be His witnesses and to reach our Jerusalem, Judea, Samaria and the ends of the earth.

If this seems completely out of reach, let's remember that we are still empowered by the same Spirit as these early believers. They were just ordinary men and women like us, but filled with the indefatigable Holy Spirit. Our Jerusalem, Judea and Samaria are within relatively easy grasp. We may not all go to the ends of the earth, but we can certainly have an 'ends of the earth' mindset. That means being well-informed and praying for unreached peoples and those seeking to share the gospel with them. Some of us also have the privilege of living in multicultural towns and cities where 'unreached' peoples have turned up on our doorstep! We don't even have to face the inconvenience of arduous travel! Befriending overseas students, immigrants or refugees can create ideal opportunities to introduce them to the Saviour.

We also have one *huge* advantage over these early followers of Jesus – we have the complete Bible in many different languages. So, with the Bible in our hands, the Holy Spirit of power, love and self-control in our hearts and filled with God's love for the lost, we become an unstoppable force for God's kingdom in this world! We need to start where we are and trust God to open doors before us as He chooses, just as He did for Paul and his co-workers. The Acts of the Apostles is finished, but we have the scary, amazing privilege of continuing those acts!

Notes
1. Christine Platt, *Acts 1–12: Church on the move*, Cover to Cover Bible Study series (Farnham: CWR, 2010).
2. Ajith Fernando, *The NIV Application Commentary: Acts* (Grand Rapids: Zondervan, 1998) p40–41.

WEEK | ONE

WEEK ONE
Let's go!

Opening Icebreaker

What are some words you would use to describe the apostle Paul?

Bible Readings

- Acts 13 and 14
- Matthew 28:18–20

Opening our Eyes

The leadership team in the Antioch church was racially and socially varied, reflecting the diversity of the city's population. Too often we find church leadership is monocultural, monoracial and of similar age group, whereas the communities they serve reveal a rich mixture of people groups. Then we wonder why our churches are not reaching into every facet of our communities.

The Antioch church was born out of missionary activity (Acts 11) and it demonstrated its kingdom vision by being willing to release its best for the further expansion of the gospel. They took Jesus' words to heart: 'Therefore go' (Matt. 28:19–20). How hard it sometimes seems to be for us to think beyond our own community and be willing to gift our resources – people and finances – to go to other unreached areas. Maybe a key to this was that worship and seeking God's face and will were clearly a priority for the believers in Antioch.

The incident with Bar-Jesus (Acts 13:6–12) is salutary for any who engage in pioneer activity and/or experience opposition in seeking to do God's work. The Holy Spirit showed Paul that this was no time for tolerance. The enemy needed to be unmasked. Satan overreached himself and the resulting miracle was proof enough for Sergius Paulus to come to faith. Opposition is to be expected when we aim to bring the light of Jesus into the dark places of Satan's kingdom.

As the journey progressed, the leadership passed from Barnabas to Paul. Barnabas was not threatened or offended. As long as God's work was done he was content, even if it meant playing second fiddle.

Thus, a church-planting pattern begins to emerge:
- They go to unreached places

Let's go!

- They preach in synagogues to Jews and God-fearing Gentiles
- There is a response – sometimes massive, sometimes mixed
- They teach the new converts and establish churches
- Opposition arises – when it gets too explosive they leave for another place
- Later they return to strengthen the disciples and appoint leaders
- They return to home base

It is interesting to note the teaching they gave to these new believers (Acts 14:21–22). They encouraged them to remain true to the faith, and they warned them of the inevitability of hardships. Is that what we focus on with new believers? Do we warn them that they have an enemy? They also prayed and entrusted these fledgling churches to God. Paul and Barnabas trusted God to look after them. They had done their part and it was now time to move on. That's faith!

John Stott points out Paul's 'extraordinary versatility… in adapting himself to different situations; he appeared to be equally at ease with individuals and crowds, Jews and Gentiles, the religious and the irreligious, the educated and the uneducated, the friendly and the hostile'.[1]

One example of this is when speaking to pagans he did not refer to the Old Testament Scriptures of which they were ignorant, but talked of the natural world which was familiar to them (Acts 14:15–17). In today's developed world many people are without knowledge of God's Word and consider Him irrelevant to their daily life. But they are hungry for love, community and some sense of personal significance – all of which can only truly be found in the gospel. How can we follow Paul's example and thus really connect with the felt needs of those around us?

Acts 13–28

Discussion Starters

1. Identify the diversity of the leadership team in the Antioch church.

2. What are the advantages and disadvantages of having a diverse leadership team?

3. How would you describe the church in Antioch?

4. What was involved in Sergius Paulus coming to faith?

5. What can we learn from this incident for our own lives and witness?

Let's go!

6. What do we learn about Paul from his message in the synagogue at Pisidian Antioch?

_____
_____
_____
_____

7. What do we learn about Paul and Barnabas from their encounter with the crowd in Lystra?

_____
_____
_____
_____

8. What are the main concerns of your unbelieving friends, family and work colleagues?

_____
_____
_____
_____

9. How could you demonstrate Jesus to them by action and speech in ways they could accept and understand?

_____
_____
_____
_____

WEEK | ONE

Personal Application

What is 'the work' to which God has called you in terms of building His kingdom (Acts 13:2)? Family, friends, workmates, neighbours – these are obvious people with whom to start. Who has God specifically put on your heart to pray for and demonstrate Jesus to? Do you need to take some time to worship, pray and fast to get on His wavelength for the people in your world?

Be on your guard, the enemy of souls will hate this. Expect opposition for 'we are not unaware of his schemes' (2 Cor. 2:11). Take encouragement from Paul and Barnabas, who, despite heavy opposition, 'were filled with joy and with the Holy Spirit' (Acts 13:52), knowing they were following the footsteps of the Master.

Seeing Jesus in the Scriptures

In this missionary journey we see a demonstration of the heart of Jesus. He 'came to seek and to save what was lost' (Luke 19:10). He was the first and most effective cross-cultural missionary. He left all that was familiar and beautiful. He left loving relationships and came to this broken world of misery, pain and rejection. We can't conceive of the vast gulf He had to cross. No barrier or difference we face comes close to what He endured. And He did it all in love and mercy.

We are called to follow in His footsteps. Some of us will cross continents. Others will cross cultures in their own nation. Some of us will cross the street. Jesus goes before us, still seeking to save what was lost.

Notes
1. John Stott, *The Message of Acts*, *The Bible Speaks Today* series (Leicester: IVP, 1990) p218.

WEEK TWO
Disaster averted

Opening Icebreaker

What ways has God used to guide you in big decisions?

Bible Readings

- Acts 15:1–16:10
- Ephesians 2:1–22

Acts 13–28

Opening our Eyes

At first glance, a debate about circumcision seems irrelevant to us today. In reality it highlights the ongoing human tendency to want to add something to Jesus' work of salvation, rather than humbly acknowledging that we are saved by grace through faith alone (Eph. 2:8–9).

Some Jewish Christians of the Pharisees group had a problem: how could Gentiles be saved if they didn't obey Moses' law and get circumcised? This led on to another issue: how could Jewish Christians fellowship with Gentile believers who didn't follow Moses' laws about food?

This controversy disturbed the church at Antioch, so the leaders made a wise decision. They sent a high-level delegation to the apostles and leaders in the Jerusalem church. It's instructive to note how the leaders dealt with this conflict. God knew that succeeding generations would need all the help they could get when faced with church conflicts.

The meeting seems to have been open to everyone and all could have their say. All seemed to listen to one another. The leaders then met together. Peter reminded them of his experience with Cornelius and his household and how God had given them the Holy Spirit. Paul and Barnabas gave testimony of how God had worked among the Gentiles. James then summarised and related Old Testament Scripture to the issue.

James was the acknowledged leader of the meeting. He was the younger brother of Jesus. His nickname was 'Old Camel Knees' because he spent so much time in prayer. He followed Jewish customs rigorously, but didn't impose them on others. He wasn't the leader because he was Jesus' brother, but because he was an outstanding man.[1] With Mary and Joseph as parents and Jesus as big brother, he certainly had a godly start in life! (He was stoned to death in AD 62.)

James then suggested a compromise – not in the matter of salvation, but in day-to-day interaction between believers of Jewish and Gentile background so as not to offend. The ensuing letter was received with immense joy and relief by Gentile believers. It healed the potential chasm facing the Early Church. We, today, also need to guard the theology of salvation by grace alone, and not add any 'extras', such as doing good, faithful attendance at church or other man-made rules, eg abstaining from alcohol or smoking. We need to clearly distinguish between the fruit of a life with Christ and the basis of it.

Another conflict arose! This time between Paul and Barnabas. Barnabas, ever the encourager, wanted to give Mark another chance. Paul thought it was too risky, so they parted. Division is never desirable, but God can use it, as He did in this instance. The missionary endeavour went in two directions – Asia Minor and Cyprus. Barnabas was eventually proved right to believe in Mark, which Paul later acknowledged (2 Tim. 4:11).

Paul set off with Silas and recruited young Timothy in Lystra. After all that fuss about circumcision not being necessary, Paul had Timothy circumcised. Why? There are times when we need to surrender our freedom in order not to hinder relationships.

God promises to guide, but it isn't always straightforward. Paul's team made their plans and God stopped them in various ways. But they didn't become paralysed, they kept moving on. God can guide a moving team more easily than one which is stuck. In Troas they recruited Luke (Acts 16:10 'we') and received the call to Europe.

Acts 13–28

Discussion Starters

1. Why is it that humans want to add something to Jesus' work on the cross in order to receive salvation?
   _____
   _____
   _____

2. What are some symptoms that show we are not fully trusting Christ for salvation, but are trusting in our own works as well?
   _____
   _____
   _____

3. What are some symptoms that show we are fully trusting Christ for salvation?
   _____
   _____
   _____

4. How can we grow in our conviction that salvation is by faith alone?
   _____
   _____
   _____

5. What can we learn from the conflict situation we have just read about in the Early Church?
   _____
   _____
   _____

6. What can we learn about Barnabas from his relationships with Paul and Mark?

7. How do you think Mark felt about his relationship with Paul and Barnabas?

8. How can you encourage others when they fail?

9. What freedoms might you need to surrender so as not to hinder God speaking through you? (See 1 Cor. 10:23–11:1.)

10. How would you describe the response of Paul's team to the Holy Spirit's guidance? (See also Prov. 16:9.)

Acts 13-28

Personal Application

It's disappointing when we are thwarted in our plans, and it is tempting to push on come what may. If Paul and his team had done that, God's purposes for Europe would have been compromised. We need to keep a balance between running our race in faith and not giving up at the first obstacle, but also recognising when we need to surrender our plans and look for where God is leading us. How gracious God is to give us His Holy Spirit as our constant companion and guide.

> Trust in the LORD with all your heart and lean not on your own understanding; in all your ways acknowledge him, and he will make your paths straight.
>
> Proverbs 3:5–6

Seeing Jesus in the Scriptures

'We have been made holy by the sacrifice of the body of Jesus Christ once for all' (Heb. 10:10). Let that truth roll around in your mind. It is written in the passive tense – you 'have been made holy'. This means that you had nothing to do with it. You just had to let it be done to you. When God looks at you, He sees the holiness of His Son. Our daily reality is that God is at work in us, changing us to be restored to our true status of holiness (Phil. 1:6).

> How deep the Father's love for us,
> How vast beyond all measure.
> That He should give His only Son
> To make a wretch His treasure.[2]

Notes
1. William Barclay, *The Acts of the Apostles*, revised edition (Westminster: John Knox Press) p115. Quoted in Robert C. Girard, series ed. Larry Richards, *The Book of Acts*, *The Smart Guide to the Bible* series (Thomas Nelson, 2007. GRQ Inc.) p182.
2. From 'How Deep the Father's Love' by Stuart Townend; used by permission. (For full details, see copyright page.)

WEEK THREE

Europe responds to the gospel

Opening Icebreaker

How has God encouraged you during tough times?

Bible Readings

- Acts 16:11–18:22
- Galatians 3:26–29

Acts 13–28

Opening our Eyes

Paul's second missionary journey took an unexpected turn. God graced this earth with His physical presence in Israel. His Church was born in Jerusalem and missionary activity had been limited to parts of Asia. God always has broader horizons in view. Greece, as the gateway to Europe, was the next step. Paul and his team wasted no time in further debate. God has said it, so they 'got ready at once' (Acts 16:10) – eager, instant obedience.

Luke highlights the stories of three founding members of the church in Philippi: Lydia, a successful business woman, a slave-girl delivered from demonic oppression[1] and a prison officer – probably all Gentiles. God brought these disparate people together in Himself in direct contradiction to the Jewish male's regular prayer, where he thanks God that he is not a Gentile, a woman or a slave. Through this God shows that all man-made walls of separation are broken down. He accepts all who believe (Gal. 3:26–28).

More opposition led to Paul and Silas being imprisoned. Despite having been stripped, flogged and dumped in a dark, dank cell with their feet jammed in stocks, they pray and sing hymns. They demonstrate to the other prisoners and jailer that God has filled them with joy (Psa. 16:11). They see everywhere God sends them as a mission field. As the ground lurched and chains fell off, everyone knew that mighty God had come to the party!

Paul and Silas seemed to have carried out the first recorded 'sit-in' (Acts 16:37). They stood up for their rights for the sake of the Philippian church and its future legality, not because of hurt pride.

Still convinced of God's call to Greece, the team was not discouraged at being expelled from Philippi, but journeyed on to Thessalonica – only to experience similar hostility. However, the Bereans were a breath of fresh air (Acts 17:11). Paul seemed to be the lightning rod for Jewish opposition, so again he had to escape and went to Athens. (I might have been tempted to go home at that point!) Whereas God can use circumstances to guide us in different directions, Paul clung to God's clear call to Macedonia and until God said otherwise, he persevered.

In Athens, Paul was 'greatly distressed' by all the idols. But he used this positively in his evangelistic message: 'I see that in every way you are very religious' (Acts 17:22). When we encounter people with starkly different values and belief systems, rather than coming up against them, let's try to find a way to connect and lead on to being able to present the gospel.

From 1 Corinthians 2:3 we learn that Paul went to Corinth in 'weakness and fear, and with much trembling'. What lay ahead? Persecution, beatings, rejection? He knew that the Corinthians were full of pride and immorality, hooked on the pursuit of pleasure and sex. 'Preaching Christ crucified' (1 Cor. 2:2) would bring him into direct opposition to these values. How tender of God to give him further reassurance of His presence and protection (Acts 18:9–10).

When the synagogue closed its doors, God opened an interesting alternative (Acts 18:7). Imagine the stir that was caused when Crispus, the synagogue ruler and his whole family, believed in Jesus, left the synagogue and joined the next-door congregation!

Finally, in Corinth God provided a settled base for ministry from where Paul and his team were able to establish the Corinthian church which still exists to this day. Paul also wrote his two letters to the Thessalonians.

Acts 13-28

Discussion Starters

1. What was involved in Lydia's 'instant' conversion?

2. How can we work with God in preparing people to receive and respond to His good news?

3. Facing adversity with joy and peace is a powerful demonstration of the reality of God. How can you grow in this area and encourage others in difficulties?

4. How can you follow the example of the Bereans? (Acts 17:11.)

Europe responds to the gospel

WEEK THREE

5. Paul used the altar inscription 'To an unknown God' as a connection to share the gospel. What were the main points of his talk?

---

6. What points of connection to the gospel can you find for your circle of friends, neighbours and family?

---

7. What are the advantages and disadvantages of 'tent making', eg earning your own living while being actively involved in ministering to others?

---

8. Paul made a vow, possibly to thank God for His protection. How can 'vows' help us today in our walk with God?

Acts 13–28

Personal Application

A witness tells what they have seen or heard. What have you seen and heard of Jesus this week? For what specific things are you asking Him? Do you write these down and remember to thank Him for His answers, whatever they might be? You may not have a dramatic deliverance or healing to report, but Jesus is King of minutiae as well as majestic miracles. Bring Him into every area of life and you'll find you have ample evidence to be His witness.

> Count your blessings, name them one by one,
> Count your blessings, see what God hath done!
> Count your blessings, name them one by one,
> And it will surprise you what the Lord hath done.[2]

Seeing Jesus in the Scriptures

Evangelism is never straightforward or easy. It's an assault on Satan's kingdom and he doesn't let anyone go without a titanic struggle. He uses various strategies to keep us dumb and ineffective – fear, inadequacy, outright hostility, but 'the one who is in [us] is greater than the one who is in the world' (1 John 4:4). Be assured you are on the winning side. On the cross Jesus won the victory and Satan was and remains a defeated foe.

We can confidently take hold of the victorious power of Jesus in our trembling hands and be strengthened to be His witnesses in every area of our daily lives. His promise to Paul is also His promise to us: 'I am with you' (Acts 18:10).

Notes
1. John Stott, *The Message of Acts*, The Bible Speaks Today series (Leicester: IVP, 1990) p270: 'I think Luke means us to understand that she was converted as well as delivered.'
2. The refrain from the hymn 'Count Your Blessings' by Johnson Oatman, Jr (1856–1922).

WEEK FOUR
WEEK FOUR
The persecuted Church blossoms

Opening Icebreaker

In what ways does the Church suffer persecution in today's world?

Bible Readings

- Acts 18:23–21:16
- Luke 9:22–24,51,62

Opening our Eyes

Paul's church-planting heart prompted him to undertake a third missionary journey. His aim was to strengthen the existing believers and establish solid local leadership so that these churches could stand strong and reach out to the regions beyond.

Meanwhile Paul's co-workers, Priscilla and Aquila, used tact, gentleness and courage to correct the gifted and enthusiastic Apollos, who was teaching an incomplete message. His humility in accepting this correction enabled God to richly bless his future ministry (Acts 18:28; 1 Cor. 3:6).

The Ephesian Twelve also had incomplete knowledge. They were disciples of John and had repented, but had no faith in Jesus nor had they received the Holy Spirit. This was not a two-stage conversion experience.[1]

Ephesus was a hotbed of occult practices and superstition, and became an area of intense spiritual warfare. God turned Satan's machinations to His own triumph. As proof of repentance people burned their costly occult scrolls. Satan then stirred up greed and fear in the business community and again God used secular authorities to defend His people. As John Stott says: 'the impartiality of Gallio, the friendship of "officials" and the cool reasonableness of the city clerk combined to give the gospel freedom to continue on its victorious course.'[2]

Paul spoke first to the God-fearing in the synagogue and then to the secular in private homes and a lecture hall. It is estimated that over two years, he spoke and answered questions from 11.00am to 4.00pm (the hottest part of the day). This totalled 3,120 hours of gospel explanation. Many visitors came to Ephesus, were convinced and took the gospel back to their home areas.

Paul stayed five years in Corinth and Ephesus. This was long-term 'sowing' of the Word. This settled ministry also gave him the time and space to write his theological treatise – the letter to the Romans.

After this long visit he recognised that his work was done and he could safely leave the churches in God's care and under local leadership. The farewells were emotional. Paul did not keep himself emotionally detached as he taught the people. He gave himself heart and soul for their encouragement and strengthening.

Paul was convinced the Holy Spirit had told him to go to Jerusalem and that suffering awaited him there. When the Spirit relayed the same message to Agabus and other friends, they interpreted it as a warning for Paul not to go. John Stott points out that we need 'to draw a distinction between a prediction and a prohibition'.[3] In their love for Paul, his friends understandably wanted him to avoid pain. This echoes Peter's rebuke to Jesus when He spoke of His coming suffering. Jesus turned and said to Peter, 'Get behind me, Satan! You are a stumbling block to me; you do not have in mind the things of God, but the things of men' (Matt. 16:23).

In our legitimate concern for others do we sometimes try to deflect them from the path of God's calling on their lives? It seems that his friends' concern only made it harder for Paul to turn his face steadfastly towards Jerusalem and the trials that awaited him. Yet he was clear in his mind and heart about what God had said to him, and nothing would be allowed to stand in his way. He was willing to pay the ultimate price whenever God called him to do so.

Acts 13-28

Discussion Starters

1. What characterised Priscilla and Aquila's ministry?

2. What four things were necessary for the Ephesian Twelve to become true believers in Christ?

3. What was the result of people misusing the name of Jesus (Acts 19:13–20)?

4. The new converts burned their occult scrolls as proof of their repentance and repudiation of anything that could hinder their walk with Christ. Is there anything you need to 'burn' that is holding you back from full surrender to Christ?

The persecuted Church blossoms

5. What motivations to persevere do we learn about in Paul's life from his farewell to the Ephesian elders?

6. Which of these motivations could help you in your life?

7. How can we hear the voice of the Spirit?

8. Why was there such a difference between the way Paul interpreted the Spirit's words and the way others did?

9. What can we learn from the fact that Luke mentions Philip's four daughters who prophesied (Acts 21:9)?

Acts 13–28

Personal Application

It can be easier to deal with a short, sharp crisis than an ongoing, prolonged trial. We have to dig deep into our faith reserves to persevere for the long haul. Paul sets us a good example. He knew that God's call on his life would engender suffering and had resolved to meet it with faith.

How about you? Much of the developed world is suffering-averse, yet we are called to a life of self-denial. In a culture which craves comfort and entertainment, saying 'no' to yourself seems crazy, but it is the way to the abundant life that Jesus promises (John 10:10). In what ways is God asking you to deny yourself for the sake of the kingdom?

Seeing Jesus in the Scriptures

If self-denial seems too hard, focus on Jesus. He denied Himself the pleasures of heaven for a time, the normal joys of family life, a settled home and income, His reputation and approval by others. Many of His people have followed that same road, and have entered into a reward beyond their wildest dreams which amply makes up for any privations they endured (1 Cor. 2:9; 2 Cor. 4:17). Jesus said: 'Anyone who intends to come with me has to let me lead. You're not in the driver's seat – I am. Don't run from suffering; embrace it. Follow me and I'll show you how. Self-help is no help at all. Self-sacrifice is the way, *my* way, to finding yourself, your true self' (Luke 9:23–24, *The Message*).

Notes
1. John Stott, *The Message of Acts, The Bible Speaks Today* series (Leicester: IVP, 1990) p304.
2. Ibid, p311.
3. Ibid, p333.

WEEK FIVE
Faith under fire

Opening Icebreaker

What are some Bible verses which express the importance of unity?

Bible Readings

- Acts 21:17–23:35
- 1 Corinthians 9:19–23

Acts 13-28

Opening our Eyes

James and the Jerusalem elders were preoccupied by a thorny issue – namely Paul! They'd probably had a few sleepless nights and several leadership team meetings. Yet they received him warmly and listened attentively to his detailed report. They praised God when they heard how Europe had responded to the gospel, that the Athenian philosophers now knew who their unknown God was, that believers' lives in Corinth were being transformed and that many in Ephesus had burned their occult paraphernalia.

Gently and tactfully they drew the conversation to the problem and offered a solution (Acts 21:20-25). Everyone's aim was to maintain unity and they were prepared to pay a high price for it. They were not compromising their convictions, but seeking an accommodation of sensitivities.

Unfortunately, through the intransigence of Jewish opposition the peace plan backfired. Several commentators point out that the action of shutting the Temple gates in 21:30 is a symbol of the Jewish leaders and people shutting their minds to God and His messenger. The Temple was now ripe for destruction, which happened in AD 70, less than a decade later.

Again Roman justice saved Paul from being torn limb from limb. Despite all the aggression, being bruised and shaken, and although called by God as the apostle to the Gentiles, Paul never lost his heart concern for the salvation of the Jews (Rom. 10:1). He pleaded for the opportunity to speak to the crowd.

His testimony is a model for us. He explained his background – who he was, how he met Jesus and how his life had changed since. Amazingly the crowd listened quietly, and then came the inflammatory words 'God sent me to the Gentiles' and it was all on again. His next inflammatory word was 'resurrection'. Why was this such a biggie? For the Jews, to believe in the resurrection of Jesus would mean they would have to accept that He was who He claimed to be – God come to earth to forgive sinners – their promised Messiah, whom they had killed.

Ananias the high priest – the one who had spiritual responsibility for the people Paul loved – was known to be corrupt and violent. He was removed from office a year later and assassinated in AD 66. For reasons of His own, God sometimes allows evil people to exercise influence and leadership for a while, but eventually they receive their punishment. In these trying circumstances God's people need to lean on almighty God in faith, trusting His timetable.

Paul could have felt really discouraged. His words engendered only anger and rebellion instead of repentance and faith. His hopes and dreams that his Jewish 'family' would recognise their Saviour lay in ruins at his feet. Jesus knew Paul needed a boost (Acts 23:11), and what a wonderful boost he received!

God also made sure that the plot of the fanatics became known, and Paul was spirited away from danger. It's ironic that one smallish man was given a huge armed escort by the Roman authorities! This could also be a picture of the spiritual armies that surround God's people (2 Kings 6:15–17). Paul was protected because of Roman citizenship. God's people are protected because of their heavenly citizenship. Now, stuck in the dungeon of Herod's palace in Caesarea, Paul is left to wonder how God is going to get him to Rome as He had promised.

Acts 13–28

Discussion Starters

1. Why did some of the believing Jews have a problem with Paul? (See Acts 21:20–21.)

2. Was their accusation true?

3. What solution was proposed by James and the elders?

4. What was Paul's motivation in agreeing to this?

5. Are there any situations where you need to 'accommodate' in order to maintain unity?

Faith under fire

WEEK FIVE

6. Read again Paul's testimony – Acts 22:1–21.
a) What was Paul's attitude when speaking to the crowd?

b) What was his life like before he met Christ?

c) Why did he stress these things?

d) What did he give the most attention to – who he was before, how he met Christ or how his life changed?

e) Would his hearers have understood how to become a believer in Christ by listening to Paul's testimony?

f) How had his life changed?

7. Describe the three visions that Paul received.
(See Acts 22:6–10,17–21; 23:11.)

8. What effect did these visions have on Paul?

9. What significant experiences with Jesus could you look back on for encouragement when your faith is tested?

Acts 13–28

Personal Application

Paul was ready to take any opportunity to share his story with unbelievers. For him, the most vital thing in the world was that people should know the truth about Jesus and respond to His invitation to belong to His family. How about you? Are you ready to share your story?

Go back over Question 6, relating to Paul's testimony. Write out your own story, paying particular attention to points a, d and e. Seek out a trusted Christian friend and 'try out' your testimony on them. It may not be as dramatic as Paul's, but it is your unique story and that is powerful in itself.

Pray for opportunities to share your story, and trust that God will use it.

Seeing Jesus in the Scriptures

Jesus revealed Himself in visions to Paul three times. Maybe not all of us will receive a vision like his in our earthly lifetime, but Jesus constantly reveals Himself to us through His Word, through creation (Psa. 19:1–4; Rom. 1:20) and through people. But sometimes we miss Him by being too busy or distracted. We need to stop regularly and be attentive to Him.

Thank You, Lord Jesus, that You want to communicate with us. Help us to be alert to any ways in which You are revealing Yourself.

WEEK SIX
Interacting with movers and shakers

Opening Icebreaker

What Christians do you know of who exert a positive influence in the media or politics? Pray for them.

Bible Readings

- Acts 24, 25 and 26
- Colossians 4:5–6
- 1 Peter 3:15–16

Opening our Eyes

Paul found himself up against the Jewish religious legal system as well as the Roman one. How did he feel about that? From his responses it seems he was already formulating the theology expressed in Colossians 4:5–6. These stressful, high-powered encounters were actually opportunities to talk about the Saviour he loved and served. It would appear he prayed for wisdom to know 'how to answer everyone' rather than asking God for a 'Get out of jail' card.

Although he could relate to all types of people, his background and education ideally equipped him to communicate on an intellectual and social level with high-flyers. He relished the opportunity to speak into their minds and hearts. Paul was competent and respectful in defending himself, as was Stephen before him (Acts 6:8–10; 7:1–60). Both understood where their opponents were coming from and tried to help them grow in their understanding of God's ways and, particularly in this instance, how Jesus was the fulfillment of the Messianic promises in the Old Testament. We also need to understand the questions, viewpoints and criticisms held by the world so that we can formulate answers and be ready to share them with 'gentleness and respect' (1 Pet. 3:15).

It's easy to go on answering questions that people were asking ten to twenty years ago, but we need to engage with our present culture, however painful or frustrating that may be for us. For example, we can use our discernment when we watch TV or read a contemporary novel or listen to song lyrics (if we can hear them!) and seek to evaluate the messages that are being transmitted. What is it that stirs the hearts of those who have not yet acknowledged God and responded to His invitation to relationship?

We need more 'Pauls' and 'Paulines' today to reach people in the higher echelons of society who will be in a position to exert a broad influence in their specific spheres. People like William Wilberforce and Rosa Parks. Much Christian effort goes towards helping the poorest of the poor. That is right – we follow Jesus' example. But Jesus also reached out to the wealthy and influential – Zacchaeus (Luke 19:2–10) and the rich young man (Matt. 19:16–22). It seems harder for the well-endowed to bow the knee, but they still need the opportunity to hear (vv23–26).

An accusation often hurled against the Church is that it is 'full of hypocrites'. Sadly, in some cases that is true. So, along with getting on the wavelength of others and being able to answer questions, our lifestyle needs to back up our words. Paul strove always to keep his conscience clear before God and man (Acts 24:16). That implies making every effort all the time, as an athlete would while preparing for the Olympics. There are no days off in our walk with God.

Fortunately for all of us, to 'strive' doesn't mean that Paul or we always succeed. God's grace and forgiveness cover our mistakes and sins. But people need to see that reality – not a 'pretend holiness' that is barely skin deep. It's humbling to admit our faults and failures, but that's how we 'keep our conscience clear before God and man'. Yes, we make every effort. Yes, we fail. Yes, we come to God for forgiveness and – hallelujah! – yes, we can get up again and continue. Being honest about our failures so that people know who we truly are, warts and all, is authentic Christianity, and that realness gives people hope.

Discussion Starters

1. What was the content of Paul's interaction with Felix?

2. What was Felix's response?

3. Why did he respond that way?

4. What does Felix's response teach us about evangelism?

5. Why is it important to share our failures and pain as well as our successes and joys in all our interactions with others, whether evangelistic or with believers? (See Matt. 26:36–38; 1 Cor. 2:1–5.)

Interacting with movers and shakers

6. What can hinder us in being real with others?

7. What are some guidelines about sharing failures and sorrows with others?

8. What's involved in keeping one's conscience clear before God and man?

Personal Application

Do you know any 'Pauls' or 'Paulines' – people who are already – or have the potential to become – those who exert a broad influence in this world? Or maybe it's you? If God has equipped you or people you know with gifts and capacities that need to be developed, don't hold back. Encourage others to really go for it.

The Early Church would have been a much poorer entity if Paul had decided to deny his potential and calling and limit himself to making tents.

How can you encourage and spur yourself and others on to be all that God intends for you to be? Ask God to expand your horizons and dreams for yourself and for others. Maybe there is a young person you could pray for and possibly mentor.

Seeing Jesus in the Scriptures

From the very beginning God gave the most magnificent, stupendous promise to humanity – King Jesus was on His way (Gen. 3:15)! God gave that promise at a time when humanity had badly let Him down. The promised one would enable people to have their eyes opened, to turn from darkness to light, from the power of Satan to God, to receive forgiveness of sins and the certainty of an eternal home in heaven. Hallelujah! What a Saviour! Throughout the ages God repeated that promise (Isa. 9:6–7) and when the time was ripe He fulfilled it.

Because King Jesus came in fulfilment of God's promise, all the other divine promises are 'Yes' in Him (2 Cor. 1:20), so we can rest confidently knowing that what God says, He will do.

WEEK | SEVEN

WEEK SEVEN

God's in charge!

Opening Icebreaker

How have you or others you know experienced God's overruling in situations that you felt were going badly wrong?

Bible Readings

- Acts 27 and 28
- Philippians 1:12–14
- 2 Timothy 4:7

Acts 13-28

Opening our Eyes

Because Paul had appealed to Caesar, Festus and Agrippa were compelled by Roman law to send him to Rome. They were not at liberty to release him even though they knew he was innocent. God had promised Paul that he would testify in Rome and stand trial before Caesar (Acts 23:11; 27:23–24), so Paul's eyes were firmly fixed on that goal. He had already written his magnificent letter to the Roman Christians, whom he had probably heard about from Aquila and Priscilla. He longed to see them and was eager to preach the gospel there (Rom. 1:11,15).

Paul was an experienced sea passenger and had already been through three shipwrecks. He knew that sailing so late in the year was dangerous, but he also trusted God to get him safely to Rome. That faith was severely tested. The horrendous storm rendered his plight completely hopeless, but Paul clung on to God's promise.

The centurion Julius ignored Paul's advice at first, but later realised that he was in the presence of a man who knew what he was talking about. Paul's leadership was a key element in everyone being saved. His faith was infectious – all the dispirited passengers and crew were encouraged (Acts 27:36). His faith enabled God to use him as an agent of hope.

On board ship the centurion Julius was very kind to Paul even though he was a prisoner. When the bedraggled passengers and crew collapsed exhausted on the beach at Malta, the locals cared for them far beyond the call of duty.

Once on Malta, Paul made himself useful by collecting wood for the fire and then bringing healing to Publius' father and others. These three months on the island seem to have been a peaceful, fruitful, happy interlude. Had God responded to some searching hearts and 'arranged' the shipwreck?

God's in charge!

WEEK | SEVEN

The Roman believers came to meet Paul. What an encouragement that must have been to him!

Paul's first thought was to meet with the Jewish leaders. As usual, some believed, others resisted. Despite all the persecution he'd received Paul never gave up on the Jewish race as a whole. Luke stresses this ministry to Jews and doesn't even mention Paul's witness to the palace guard – a rotation of soldiers chained to Paul 24/7 who all heard the gospel (Phil. 1:12–14).[1]

Whereas in Acts a major teaching point is that Gentiles don't need to become Jews to be saved, in our day we need to remember that Jews don't need to become Gentiles when they embrace Christ. Many become 'fulfilled' or 'messianic' Jews, thus retaining their essential Jewishness.[2] How much of our prayer and witness is turned towards Jewish people?

Paul was an incorrigible activist, yet he had been through four and half years of inactivity as a prisoner. How did he use his time? In Rome he wrote letters to the Ephesians, Philippians and Colossians – letters that convey joy, peace, patience and contentment. He truly learned to trust God's sovereignty.

Many scholars think that Paul was released after two years, then made another journey throughout Asia and possibly Spain. He was later re-arrested and martyred in Rome AD 67/68.

As an older man he wrote: 'I have fought the good fight, I have finished the race, I have kept the faith' (2 Tim. 4:7). Let us resolve that from today we will do the same.

Acts 13–28

Discussion Starters

1. Why was Paul so keen to get to Rome?
   _____
   _____
   _____
   _____

2. How did God strengthen Paul's faith?
   _____
   _____
   _____
   _____

3. Apart from the storm, what other obstacles did Paul and the other passengers face on this journey?
   _____
   _____
   _____
   _____

4. In what ways was Paul an agent of hope for his fellow travellers?
   _____
   _____
   _____
   _____

5. In what ways could you be an agent of hope to those around you?
   _____
   _____
   _____
   _____

God's in charge!

WEEK SEVEN

6. What miracles did God do on the island of Malta?

7. What was Paul's attitude towards the Jewish people? (See also Rom. 1:16; 9:1–5; 10:1.)

8. What part do Gentiles play in the salvation of the Jews? (See Rom. 11:11–24.)

Personal Application

Paul is the major player through these chapters and it is easy to feel a bit intimidated by him – his passion and gifts seem extraordinary. However, his ministry would have been much less effective without his back-up teams – Aquila and Priscilla, Luke, Barnabas and countless others who laboured faithfully in their corner of the vineyard. No doubt they all received the commendation, 'Well done, good and faithful servant!' (Matt. 25:21) when they came face to face with Jesus in His glory.

Note that we are called to be 'good' and 'faithful' – that might not necessarily mean success as we would recognise it. Resolve from this day on to be 'good' and 'faithful' and leave the results up to God. He sees your heart.

Seeing Jesus in the Scriptures

Throughout Acts we've seen King Jesus build His Church despite all the obstacles the enemy could throw at Him. His followers took seriously His commands and promises in Matthew 28:18–20 and Acts 1:8, that they were to go and make disciples and that He would be with them. Also they would receive power to do this and spread His message over the whole world.

King Jesus is still building His Church today: 'a church so expansive with energy that not even the gates of hell will be able to keep it out' (Matt. 16:18, *The Message*). What a privilege we have to be part of such a mighty enterprise under a magnificent boss with a divine guarantee of success!

Notes
1. Robert C. Girard, series ed. Larry Richards, *The Book of Acts*, The Smart Guide to the Bible series (Thomas Nelson, 2007. GRQ Inc.) p331.
2. Ajith Fernando, *The NIV Application Commentary: Acts* (Grand Rapids: Zondervan, 1998) p629.

Leader's Notes

General note: As the Bible readings for each week are quite long, it would be good to encourage the group members to read them before coming to the group meeting.

Week One: Let's go!

Aims of the Session
1. To learn from and be inspired by Paul's and Barnabas' missionary zeal.
2. To make a practical application to reach out to those around.

Opening Icebreaker
The aim of this icebreaker is for people to assess their present understanding of Paul and then revisit this at the end of the book. Paul is a dynamic and often controversial figure and it would be good for people to gain a fuller appreciation of this hugely influential person in the growth of God's kingdom on earth.

You could make a list of what people say – try to get just words and short phrases – and go back to the list when you've finished the book, and add/modify as necessary.

Before starting the discussion you could make sure people have read the Introduction and Opening Our Eyes section. It would be useful to have a map available for these studies in order to trace the various missionary journeys. *The NIV Study Bible*[1] maps 10, 11, 12, 13 and 14 cover the relevant areas. An atlas of today's world would also be useful to identify modern country/place names.

Acts 13-28

Discussion Starters

1.
   - Barnabas – Jewish from the Jerusalem Church, originally from Cyprus.
   - Simeon called Niger – probably African.
   - Lucius – from North Africa (present-day Libya).
   - Manaen – Jewish name, 'brought up by Herod' – therefore had connections with the aristocracy.
   - Saul – Jewish, Roman citizen, from Tarsus, trained rabbi.
   - Saul and Barnabas were probably youngish – 30s. We don't know about the others.

2. Advantages:
   - More representative of the community, therefore people would feel they would be accepted and welcomed.
   - Better illustration of the kingdom – Revelation 5:9: 'every tribe and language and people and nation.'
   - Richer fellowship.
   - Disadvantages:
   - More potential for disunity and misunderstandings. They would all need to work on their relationships.
   - Possibly decision-making would take longer.

3. See Introduction. You could suggest praying these qualities into your own church or community.

4.
   - He was a seeker – God was already at work in his heart.
   - Paul and Barnabas shared God's Word with him.
   - Satan prompted Elymas to oppose God's work.
   - God gave Paul discernment to recognise the work of the enemy. God directed and empowered Paul to rebuke Elymas publicly and pronounce judgment on him.
   - God's public judgment of Elymas was the final proof to Sergius Paulus, and he came to faith. The miracle and message convinced him.

5. This is a graphic example of the spiritual battle in which we are engaged. We need to be aware of Satan's strategies (2 Cor. 2:11). Opposition must be expected but we need to remember that Satan is a defeated foe. Christ has won the victory. Therefore, we can be confident as we face daily life and seek to be His witnesses, knowing that God is already at work in people's hearts.

6.
- He had a thorough knowledge of Jewish history from Abraham to Jesus.
- He was able to quote Scripture appropriately to reinforce his message and to refute opposition.
- He must have been an eloquent and effective speaker.

NB – It would be good to emphasise that we ourselves need to know God's Word and be able to use it appropriately.

7. They were horrified that the people thought they were gods. They were determined to give all the glory to God, not take it for themselves. They spoke of God who made the natural world who blessed them materially – a contextualised message that they could understand.

8&9. It would be good to make this really practical and possible for all.

Notes
1. *The NIV Study Bible* (London, Sydney, Auckland, Toronto: Hodder & Stoughton, 1987).

Acts 13–28

Week Two: Disaster averted

Aim of the Session
1. To identify ways in which we 'add' human effort in order to 'supplement' the salvation that Christ offers. To repent of this and more fully embrace His complete and finished work of salvation.

Opening Icebreaker
The aim of this icebreaker is to help people understand that the Holy Spirit guides in different ways. We are not told all the details of how the Holy Spirit guided Paul and his team. Some means the Spirit uses are: prayer, Scripture, circumstances, peace in the heart, the advice of others – a combination of several of these is best.

Discussion Starters

1.
- Pride – we want to do something to earn it.
- Our culture pushes us in that direction. We have to prove our worth in every way.

2.
- A sense of duty in our walk with God, rather than devotion.
- Striving to please God rather than resting in His love and approval.
- Judgmental attitude to others who don't follow our particular rules.
- Hard to accept forgiveness for ourselves and extend that forgiveness to others.

3.
- Worshipful heart towards God.
- Experience joy and peace.
- Full acceptance of God's love for us and therefore acceptance of one's self – warts and all.
- Full acceptance of other people – not judgmental.
- Full enjoyment of sins forgiven.

Leader's Notes

4.
- Meditate on and learn relevant scriptures: Galatians 3:2–9,26; Ephesians 2:8–9; Titus 3:4–7.
- Make this a daily prayer of thanks to God for His immense mercy to the undeserving, ie you!
- Ask God to help you be alert to symptoms identified in Question 2 and repent.

5. The trouble came from lack of understanding in some believers in the Jerusalem church who, instead of going to the leadership with their concerns, went to the Antioch church to spread their own version of theology. These 'troublemakers' seem to have refused to listen to Paul and Barnabas. The Antioch leaders recognised they needed the Jerusalem church's wisdom (humbling for them), so sent a top-level delegation.
There was an open meeting for all – all could say their piece and all were listened to. God's Word and God's actions were given in defence of the theology. James made a sensible compromise to promote good relationships. The Jerusalem leaders wrote a letter to make sure their message was communicated accurately.

6. Barnabas could still see potential in Mark and wanted to give him a second chance. He knew that God can use flawed humanity. Even when Paul disagreed, Barnabas continued to stick up for Mark, being willing to lose the friendship and working relationship with Paul. He demonstrated costly loyalty to the younger man.

7. Deeply grateful to Barnabas and determined to do the best job possible. Probably a bit wary of Paul.

8. Keep believing in them and urging them to trust God again.

9. This could relate to what you wear, what you eat, your social activities, how you speak, anything that might make someone else stumble.

10. Seeking; Active; Surrender; Working together.

Week Three: Europe responds to the gospel

Aim of the Session
1. To give practical help and stimulus in sharing the gospel with friends, family and neighbours.

Opening Icebreaker
God used the partnership of Priscilla and Aquila when Paul was alone. He opened another door for ministry when the synagogue was effectively closed to him. He gave fruitful ministry, and also a direct word and vision.

For us, God can give specific scripture promises, the comfort of friends, peace from the Holy Spirit, and sometimes we see what God is accomplishing through the trial in our lives and others' lives.

Discussion Starters
1. She was already seeking God. Paul shared the gospel. God opened her heart. She responded. The reality of her conversion was shown in her life.
God was already at work in her life – possibly for many years. Paul had the privilege of sharing the gospel with her, and God continued His work by opening her heart. In evangelism, God is the initiator and perfector. We, His people, play an important but minor role.

Leader's Notes

2. We can engage in patient and persistent prayer. We can share our own life experience – eg answers to prayer, share helpful books, answer questions.

3.
- Listening to or singing God-inspired music communicates to deep parts of the soul when words might not hit the button.
- Reading Scripture and other Christian literature gives us examples of people who 'shone' in their troubles. These can spur us on.
- Praying with friends.
- Companionship on the journey. Paul and Silas were together. For some, asking for help and support is not easy, but loneliness can compound the suffering.

4. We need to engage heart and brain when we hear any preaching or teaching. We need to be open to what God is saying (pray for this), but also search the Scriptures.

5.
- God is knowable.
- He is the creator.
- He gives life.
- His aim is that we should seek Him and not seek the things He has made or that man has made.
- He gave a personal call to repentance.
- Jesus was raised from the dead.
- Warning of coming judgment.

6. This is not easy. Maybe someone in the group could share about a particular person and the group could share ideas. Many people are open to being prayed for even before they have any confidence in God. So, offering to pray for people can open a door for further talk about the gospel. You could also share about how God has helped you in a particular situation.

Acts 13-28

7. Advantages:
- You are in contact with everyday people who can more easily relate to an electrician or nurse than to a full-time Christian worker. This leads to more natural relationships.
- Some countries will not accept full-time missionaries.
- You can share specific work skills.
- It is less financial cost to the local church – sending a family overseas is expensive.

Disadvantages:
- Less time for personal study, language and culture study and ministry. Doing a secular job overseas can be very demanding in terms of time and energy.
- Tent makers overseas still need the backing of a local congregation, but again, this takes time. Tent makers can become isolated.

8. Making a vow or promise to God, especially if we have shared that vow with others, can strengthen our resolve when willpower is fragile. For example: we can make promises to God regarding finances, prayer and evangelism commitments, and resisting specific temptation.

Week Four: The persecuted Church blossoms

Aims of the Session
1. To learn from Priscilla and Aquila's example in ministry and character.
2. To understand more about how to hear the Spirit's voice.

Opening Icebreaker
In some areas of the world churches suffer direct persecution from government or religious authorities. Some are forced to

Leader's Notes

meet 'underground'. They risk death, torture, imprisonment and home and job loss. You could have some relevant magazines available. Some organisations are Christian Solidarity Worldwide (csw.org.uk), Open Doors (opendoorsuk.org) and Barnabas Fund (barnabasfund.org). You could take some time to pray for persecuted churches and, if you live in a freer society, you could also thank God for the freedom you experience, and ask for His continued protection of that freedom.

In more secular societies the Church can 'suffer' by being marginalised and ridiculed.

Discussion Starters

1. They had an open home – Acts 18:3,26; Romans 16:3–5. They worked and served together. They were willing to move house to serve the kingdom. They were wise, tactful, encouraging and faced danger with bravery.

2. Repentance, faith in Jesus, water baptism and the gift of the Holy Spirit.

3. The evil spirit would not yield and became very powerful. God used this power encounter to His own victory.

4. This could be any occult connections in the past or present – horoscopes, tarot cards etc. It is vital for these occult connections to be broken. You, as leader, could pray for the person, or find someone with relevant experience to pray for him or her. Also, it is good to recognise habits that distract, eg how you spend leisure time, money and energy.

5. • He was clear in the task God had given him.
• He didn't want to be guilty of anyone going to hell without being warned and instructed in how to know peace with God.

- His life was fully surrendered. Therefore, troubles and suffering did not faze him.
- He trusted God to look after His people.
- He knew he had to set a good example, as others were looking to him for leadership.

7. As an audible voice, or a sense of inner conviction, or through another person's counsel or prophecy, or through Scripture.

8. Others were swayed by their desire to protect Paul from harm. This is a very human tendency. For example, parents can seek to dissuade their children from taking steps of faith – going overseas as missionaries, changing job/location, accepting lower income for the sake of the kingdom. It is important to distinguish the Spirit's voice from the voice of natural concern. Other wise counsellors can help with this.

9. As a gift, prophecy was held in high esteem in the Early Church. In a male-dominated culture Luke takes special care to show that women have a vital part to play in the growth of the kingdom.

Week Five: Faith Under Fire

Aims of the Session
1. To understand the importance of unity and to see practical ways to promote and preserve it.
2. To learn from Paul's testimony and be ready and prepared to share one's own story.

Leader's Notes

Opening Icebreaker
The aim of this is to show that unity is to be cherished and protected. Every effort should be taken to promote and preserve it.

2 Chronicles 30:12; Psalm 133:1–3; John 17:23; Acts 4:32; Romans 15:5–6; Ephesians 4:11–13; Philippians 4:2; Colossians 2:2; 3:12–14.

Discussion Starters

1. They had been told that Paul taught the Gentiles to turn away from the law of Moses, which the Jews revered.

2. Yes, partly. Obedience to the ceremonial law of Moses was not necessary for salvation. Paul taught the Gentiles what was agreed at the Council of Jerusalem (Acts 15), so that their conduct would not be offensive to Jews – these were ceremonial laws. He would have instructed them to obey the ten commandments, but stressed that salvation was by faith in Christ alone.

3. Paul was to join in a vow and pay their expenses.

4. Paul was not averse to taking vows. He had already done so (Acts 18:18). Taking this vow, although not his intention at that time, did not conflict with his convictions about salvation by grace, so he was prepared to do it to promote unity. It was costly for him in time and financially. He also submitted to the leadership of the Jerusalem church, which should have shown his opponents that he was a loyal Jew.

5. For some this may be too personal an issue to share in a group. But you could discuss general issues like church organisation, worship style, thinking carefully about

Acts 13-28

issues before complaining, identifying which issues are really worth risking disunity over.

6. a) He was respectful, friendly and identified with them.
b) He had Jewish heritage and education. He was zealous for God, and a persecutor of Christians.
c) To identify with his hearers. He was honest and shared good things and bad things.
d) How he met Christ. That's the vital part of a testimony – not too much on life before Christ, just enough so people understand where you are coming from.
e) Yes – the important points were that he met Jesus and acknowledged Him as Lord. He was baptised and asked for forgiveness of sins in Jesus' name. He immediately obeyed Him.
f) He had been blind, now could see – both physically and spiritually. He was still zealous, but now zealous for Jesus. He understood the prophecies about Jesus in the Old Testament.

7. Conversion and commission; Warning to leave Jerusalem and go to the Gentiles; Encouragement and commission to go to Rome.

8. Awe and fear at his conversion. Direction and encouragement for his ministry. These must have strengthened Paul's faith and been significant moments on which he looked back when in difficulties.

Week Six: Interacting with movers and shakers

Aims of the Session
1. To be better equipped to share one's story of faith.

Leader's Notes

2. To grow in living an authentic Christian life – being real about struggles and failures and the reality of God's grace and empowering.

Discussion Starters

1. Paul shared his own testimony – whom he worshipped. He also spoke of right living and self-control (fruit of the Spirit), and judgment. You might want to give one or two people the opportunity to share their testimony with the group as a learning experience for everyone.

2. He wanted to hear and was interested, yet became afraid and put off deciding to follow Christ.

3. He had a spiritual interest and recognised his sinfulness. Yet, because of pride, greed and selfish ambition, he would not yield.

4. Even though the Holy Spirit was clearly at work in him (John 16:8–11), Felix resisted. Paul was an excellent communicator and passionate evangelist, yet Felix would not bow the knee. Paul didn't give up on him, but kept seeking to persuade. Even though some of our evangelistic efforts appear to bear no fruit, our responsibility is to warn and be a witness and leave the results up to God. Felix knew the truth and how to respond if and when he decided to yield to Christ's lordship.

5. We need to be real. Most people live with a mixture of happiness and sadness and regrets. They can't identify with someone pretending to be on cloud nine all the time.

6. Pride – we don't like admitting we've failed or things

aren't going well. We want people to think well of us. Some of us also have the mistaken idea that as believers we need to put on a joyous, victorious façade even when we're falling apart on the inside.

7.
- We need to be sensitive to the person's age and spiritual maturity.
- We need to trust the person – don't share with someone who is indiscreet, otherwise the whole neighbourhood will get to know!
- We don't need to wallow in the muck and mire, but rather focus on how God is helping us in it.
- We can ask the person to pray with us.

8.
- Confess sin to God as soon as we are aware of it.
- Say sorry if you've offended someone, if and when appropriate – if the person is unaware of the fault, it's usually best left unsaid.
- Ask God to search your heart so you become aware of hidden motivations or agendas (Psa. 139:23–24).
- Be increasingly responsive to the Holy Spirit's prompting.
- Make restitution if possible and appropriate.

Week Seven: God's in charge!

Aim of the Session
1. To inspire trust in God's sovereignty and promises even when situations look hopeless.

Opening Icebreaker
If the group members can't think of anything immediately, you could share personal examples or historical ones, eg John Bunyan spent 12 years in prison for his faith and yet during that time he wrote several books including *Pilgrim's*

Leader's Notes

Progress, which has had a profound effect on many people's walk with God.

Life events don't always work out as we would like. God doesn't always rescue. There are mysteries we cannot understand. But Romans 8:28 still stands – He will work good out of the most ghastly situations. We may not see it in our own lifetime. John Bunyan didn't see the full impact of his writings.

Discussion Starters

1. God had promised him that He would testify before Caesar – the most powerful man on the planet at that time. Rome was the centre of the known world. A strong church there would have a huge impact as many people travelled to Rome and then back to their homelands for trade etc. This is a key motivating factor for evangelising cities. He had also developed a great love for the Roman believers.

2. God gave him a specific promise on two occasions (Acts 23:11; 27:23–24) with a vision of Himself and also sent an angel. Paul would have seen God's kindness to him through giving him favour with Julius, and also the encouragement of having Luke and Aristarchus being willing to undertake such a dangerous journey with him. The kindness of the Maltese people would have been encouraging, and also his rescue from the snake bite.

3.
- The sailors planned to abandon them, which meant there wouldn't have been enough experienced men to know how to manage the ship.
- The soldiers planned to kill all the prisoners to prevent them from escaping.
- They had no idea where they were (Acts 27:20).
- No doubt many were seasick and too frightened to eat, so were weakened.

4. He took the role of leader. He shared God's promise with them and his faith in that promise. He set the example of eating food so they would have enough strength to swim to shore.

5. • Just 'be' with them.
   • Maintain a thankful, positive attitude.
   • Encourage people to focus on God's character – His love, mercy, power.
   • Pray for them and with them, if appropriate.
   • Do random acts of kindness.

6. He rescued Paul from the snake bite. He healed Publius' father and healed many others.

7. He recognised that the Jews were the first to receive God's laws and covenant promises and therefore should be the first to hear the gospel. He was Jewish and loved his own people. He never gave up on them as a whole race, whereas he did turn away from some individuals who rejected his message.

8. • Gentiles should be so joyful and appreciative of salvation that Jews observing them would become envious and seek salvation for themselves.
   • Gentiles should recognise that the Jews are the original 'chosen' people. Gentiles can learn much from Jews about the history of God's interactions with His people, the significance of rituals and feasts, and therefore need humble, teachable hearts towards them.
   • Gentiles should be praying for the salvation of the Jews.

NB – As a final summary of these studies, you could go back to your response to the Icebreaker in Week One, and see if you can add to or modify your initial impressions of the apostle Paul.

Notes...

 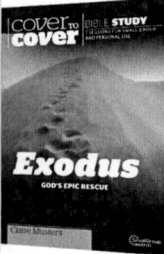  

The *Cover to Cover* Bible Study Series

1 Corinthians
Growing a Spirit-filled church
ISBN: 978-1-85345-374-8

2 Corinthians
Restoring harmony
ISBN: 978-1-85345-551-3

1,2,3 John
Walking in the truth
ISBN: 978-1-78259-763-6

1 Peter
Good reasons for hope
ISBN: 978-1-78259-088-0

2 Peter
Living in the light of God's promises
ISBN: 978-1-78259-403-1

23rd Psalm
The Lord is my shepherd
ISBN: 978-1-85345-449-3

1 Timothy
Healthy churches – effective Christians
ISBN: 978-1-85345-291-8

2 Timothy and Titus
Vital Christianity
ISBN: 978-1-85345-338-0

Abraham
Adventures of faith
ISBN: 978-1-78259-089-7

Acts 1-12
Church on the move
ISBN: 978-1-85345-574-2

Acts 13-28
To the ends of the earth
ISBN: 978-1-85345-592-6

Barnabas
Son of encouragement
ISBN: 978-1-85345-911-5

Bible Genres
Hearing what the Bible really says
ISBN: 978-1-85345-987-0

Daniel
Living boldly for God
ISBN: 978-1-85345-986-3

David
A man after God's own heart
ISBN: 978-1-78259-444-4

Ecclesiastes
Hard questions and spiritual answers
ISBN: 978-1-85345-371-7

Elijah
A man and his God
ISBN: 978-1-85345-575-9

Elisha
A lesson in faithfulness
ISBN: 978-1-78259-494-9

Ephesians
Claiming your inheritance
ISBN: 978-1-85345-229-1

Esther
For such a time as this
ISBN: 978-1-85345-511-7

Exodus
God's epic rescue
ISBN: 978-1-78951-272-4

Ezekiel
A prophet for all times
ISBN: 978-1-78259-836-7

Fruit of the Spirit
Growing more like Jesus
ISBN: 978-1-85345-375-5

Galatians
Freedom in Christ
ISBN: 978-1-85345-648-0

Genesis 1-11
Foundations of reality
ISBN: 978-1-85345-404-2

Genesis 12-50
Founding fathers of faith
ISBN: 978-1-78259-960-9

God's Rescue Plan
Finding God's fingerprints on human history
ISBN: 978-1-85345-294-9

Great Prayers of the Bible
Applying them to our lives today
ISBN: 978-1-85345-253-6

Habakkuk
Choosing God's way
ISBN: 978-1-78259-843-5

Haggai
Motivating God's people
ISBN: 978-1-78259-686-8

Hebrews
Jesus – simply the best
ISBN: 978-1-85345-337-3

Isaiah 1-39
Prophet to the nations
ISBN: 978-1-85345-510-0

Isaiah 40-66
Prophet of restoration
ISBN: 978-1-85345-550-6

Jacob
Taking hold of God's blessing
ISBN: 978-1-78259-685-1

James
Faith in action
ISBN: 978-1-85345-293-2

Jeremiah
The passionate prophet
ISBN: 978-1-85345-372-4

Job
The source of wisdom
ISBN: 978-1-78259-992-0

Joel
Getting real with God
ISBN: 978-1-78951-927-2

John's Gospel
Exploring the seven miraculous signs
ISBN: 978-1-85345-295-6

Jonah
Rescued from the depths
ISBN: 978-1-78259-762-9

Joseph
The power of forgiveness and reconciliation
ISBN: 978-1-85345-252-9

Joshua 1-10
Hand in hand with God
ISBN: 978-1-85345-542-7

Joshua 11-24
Called to service
ISBN: 978-1-78951-138-3

Judges 1-8
The spiral of faith
ISBN: 978-1-85345-681-7

Judges 9-21
Learning to live God's way
ISBN: 978-1-85345-910-8

Luke
A prescription for living
ISBN: 978-1-78259-270-9

Mark
Life as it is meant to be lived
ISBN: 978-1-85345-233-8

Mary
The mother of Jesus
ISBN: 978-1-78259-402-4

Moses
Face to face with God
ISBN: 978-1-85345-336-6

Names of God
Exploring the depths of God's character
ISBN: 978-1-85345-680-0

Nehemiah
Principles for life
ISBN: 978-1-85345-335-9

Parables
Communicating God on earth
ISBN: 978-1-85345-340-3

Philemon
From slavery to freedom
ISBN: 978-1-85345-453-0

Philippians
Living for the sake of the gospel
ISBN: 978-1-85345-421-9

Prayers of Jesus
Hearing His heartbeat
ISBN: 978-1-85345-647-3

Proverbs
Living a life of wisdom
ISBN: 978-1-85345-373-1

Psalms
Songs of life
ISBN: 978-1-78951-240-3

Revelation 1-3
Christ's call to the Church
ISBN: 978-1-85345-461-5

Revelation 4-22
The Lamb wins! Christ's final victory
ISBN: 978-1-85345-411-0

Rivers of Justice
Responding to God's call to righteousness today
ISBN: 978-1-85345-339-7

Ruth
Loving kindness in action
ISBN: 978-1-85345-231-4

Song of Songs
A celebration of love
ISBN: 978-1-78259-959-3

The Armour of God
Living in His strength
ISBN: 978-1-78259-583-0

The Beatitudes
Immersed in the grace of Christ
ISBN: 978-1-78259-495-6

The Creed
Belief in action
ISBN: 978-1-78259-202-0

The Divine Blueprint
God's extraordinary power in ordinary lives
ISBN: 978-1-85345-292-5

The Holy Spirit
Understanding and experiencing Him
ISBN: 978-1-85345-254-3

The Image of God
His attributes and character
ISBN: 978-1-85345-228-4

The Kingdom
Studies from Matthew's Gospel
ISBN: 978-1-85345-251-2

The Letter to the Colossians
In Christ alone
ISBN: 978-1-855345-405-9

The Letter to the Romans
Good news for everyone
ISBN: 978-1-85345-250-5

The Lord's Prayer
Praying Jesus' way
ISBN: 978-1-85345-460-8

The Prodigal Son
Amazing grace
ISBN: 978-1-85345-412-7

The Second Coming
Living in the light of Jesus' return
ISBN: 978-1-85345-422-6

The Sermon on the Mount
Life within the new covenant
ISBN: 978-1-85345-370-0

Thessalonians
Building Church in changing times
ISBN: 978-1-78259-443-7

The Ten Commandments
Living God's way
ISBN: 978-1-85345-593-3

The Uniqueness of our Faith
What makes Christianity distinctive?
ISBN: 978-1-85345-232-1

Zechariah
Seeing God's bigger picture
ISBN: 978-1-78951-263-2

For current prices or to order, visit **cwr.org.uk/shop**
Available online or from Christian bookshops.

Be inspired by God.
Every day.

Confidently face life's challenges by equipping yourself daily with God's Word. There is something for everyone...

Every Day with Jesus
Selwyn Hughes' renowned writing is updated by Mick Brooks into these trusted and popular notes.

Life Every Day
Jeff Lucas helps apply the Bible to daily life with his trademark humour and insight.

Inspiring Women Every Day
Encouragement, uplifting scriptures and insightful daily thoughts for women.

The Manual
Straight-talking guides to help men walk daily with God. Written by Carl Beech.

To find out more about all our daily Bible reading notes, or to take out a subscription, visit **cwr.org.uk/biblenotes** or call 01252 784700.
Also available in Christian bookshops.

SmallGroup central

All of our small group ideas and resources in one place

Online:

smallgroupcentral.org.uk is filled with free video teaching, tools, articles and a whole host of ideas.

On the road:

A range of seminars themed for small groups can be brought to your local community. Contact us at **hello@smallgroupcentral.org.uk**

In print:

Books, study guides and DVDs covering an extensive list of themes, Bible books and life issues.

Find out more at:
smallgroupcentral.org.uk

Courses and events

Waverley Abbey College

Publishing and media

Conference facilities

Transforming lives

CWR's vision is to enable people to experience personal transformation through applying God's Word to their lives and relationships.

Our Bible-based training and resources help people around the world to:
- Grow in their walk with God
- Understand and apply Scripture to their lives
- Resource themselves and their church
- Develop pastoral care and counselling skills
- Train for leadership
- Strengthen relationships, marriage and family life and much more.

Our insightful writers provide daily Bible reading notes and other resources for all ages, and our experienced course designers and presenters have gained an international reputation for excellence and effectiveness.

CWR's Training and Conference Centre in Surrey, England, provides excellent facilities in an idyllic setting – ideal for both learning and spiritual refreshment.

CWR Applying God's Word to everyday life and relationships

CWR, Waverley Abbey House,
Waverley Lane, Farnham,
Surrey GU9 8EP, UK

Telephone: +44 (0)1252 784700
Email: info@cwr.org.uk
Website: cwr.org.uk

Registered Charity No. 294387
Company Registration No. 1990308